Divine Soul Empowerment
living in the light

This work is devoted to all beings who wish to
take the path of Divine Soul Empowerment.

Precious friends who helped with the creation of this book

Gratitude is a way of being, a path that leads us to growth, joy, abundance, love and resonance with the universe. Gratitude is a prayer that is cultivated within our hearts and inspires us to give back to life the many gifts that we receive. Gratitude leads us to view life as precious and to understand that life is continually nurturing us to our fullest potential. For this we give thanks by offering life our love, compassion, joy and service.

I give thanks:

To Patricia, my lifelong friend and soul sister
who has touched this book with her beauty and light.

To my daughter, Arielle whose light and love
bring these works into reality.

To my long time friend and designer
of all my books, Dianne Rux.

To Shannon, thank you for your unique gifts
that helped bring this book into a reality.

To Deborah thank you for being the scribe of
these sacred transmissions.

Deepest gratitude to Tom, my eternal friend
whose support has made these works possible.

This book is dedicated to my beautiful daughters,
Alyssa and Arielle, whom I love and treasure beyond all words.

Blessings

With the Light you can change the world. This is the teaching of the Council of Light. For truth to become a reality, you must know yourself as a Divine Being.

We welcome you to the *Council of Light* where you will receive Holy frequencies that will heal the core of separation, opening your heart to *The Light of Being*.

Seek the Kingdom first and you will know heaven.

Namaste

Jaya

Contents

Contents

To live in love is to sail forever, spreading seeds of joy and peace in hearts.
Kindness is my only guiding star. In its light, I sail a straight route,
I have my motto written on my sail: "to live in love."
St. Therese of Lisieux

Namaste'

I honor the place in you in
which the entire universe dwells.
I honor the place in you which is of
love, of truth, of light and of peace.
When you are in that place in you,
and I am in that place in me...
We are one.

If the only prayer you ever say in your entire life
is thank you, it will be enough.
Meister Eckhart

Broken Open by Grace
The Life of Jaya Sarada

Dear Reader,

I wish to share my heart with you as you begin the journey through *Divine Soul Empowerment.*

Growing up in Ojai, California I was exposed to the ancient teachings of Theosophy and Krishnamurti. I attended a most beautiful school based on these teachings called Happy Valley. It was an extraordinary life with folk dancing, vegetarian food, nature walks, meditation and learning based on interest.

These early years planted deep seeds in my soul that went dormant as I began my journey in the world of duality. Unknown to me was the fact that deep inside was a beacon of light destined to activate when my soul lessons were learned. When learned my soul could hold the frequency of a much higher consciousness.

My mother was an earnest seeker of truth imbued with a natural silence, beauty and Divine love. My father was a hunter, a farmer and an alcoholic who was very rooted in sensual pleasure. My life was torn between the transmission of sacred truth and the conditioning of the world as my parents were split in the middle because of their values. This duality was the foundation or grace upon which I later took the path of my Spiritual awakening. I now understand that the frequency of truth, love and beauty is far more powerful than that of egoic desire, based on the false sense of self.

I was blessed to have a mother who was my spiritual teacher. I went through many years of being lost in the illusion of this world. Narcotics and alcohol were in my father's life and when I turned 16, I also turned towards my father's addictions for a few years. ▶

At some point in desperation, I crawled back to my mother with my little girl, Alyssa. My mom welcomed me home with the condition I study and learn the way of the Masters. We lived a Divine life, immersed in self-inquiry, beauty, music and most of all there was never a day without love and kindness. When I was in my early twenties my mother took me to India with the light of my life, my little girl. We lived in the ashram of Sai Baba several times over a period of 12 years. My life was forever changed from living in the ashram. I learn to sit and wait, to sing Sacred Bhajans, and I experienced unexplainable joy and peace; loving God more and more. Eventually my mom rented a large home in Bangalore, that became alive with weekly bhajans, fresh jasmine and daily home cooked vegetarian Indian food. This seed of Divine love began to sprout in the early days of India and has become the foundation for my life's awakening.

Returning to America to a "normal" life, I soon married and was blessed to give birth to a beautiful daughter, Arielle, who became another light of my life. We took many trips to India together and she also attended Waldorf and Krishanmurti schools. My daughter has been an integral part of my writing and work for over 10 years now and has blessed this book with her love, attention and writings.

My life has been so very blessed with the profound teachers that were in my mother's circle. When she married again it was to Krishnamurti's physician, Dr. Keller. Our life together became a joyous inquiry into the nature of reality. My mother transmitted such a high vibration that it was instilled in my soul. I came to yearn to know God, to know truth; a deep desire grew in me to, in some way, alleviate humanities suffering. I became a student of Acupuncture and Holistic Healing, obtaining numerous certificates in healing modalities. I also studied Transpersonal Psychology and other forms of transformational therapy.

Grace has led the way, allowing the wounds of my soul to surface and open to a greater light for long-lasting healing. This healing has been the reason for my work. I am instructed to offer a helping hand to others who have struggled with duality and loss of true essence through mistaken identity and incorrect conditioning.

I am here to share with you solutions for life's tragedies, losses, and pain. Together we can learn a new practice that invites the Divine to become a partner on your journey home; to offer the open wound to Divine healing so more light can enter your being. The wounds of the soul can be transformed through portals of Grace, so a greater love can guide your life. The only thing that is required is commitment and a devotion from your heart that aims for the target of Divine union.

Plagued with the virus of duality and separation, I have struggled in my life to find out who I am. I feel like I am not really from this world's consciousness and have endeavored to, *"Live in the world but not of it."*

I began writing my first channeled book *Trust in Yourself* after attending many satsangs on the nature of self-inquiry. My writing continued with the next book being *The Path of Return* an in-depth book about energy anatomy and ascension, then *Well-being in Body, Mind and Spirit* and *Life Essence Awakening.*

My life has been dedicated to uncovering the truth and revealing the cause of sorrow, going deep into the root of thoughts and emotions that are the underlying cause of unhappiness.

In 2014, I began channeling *The Council of Light.* The books that came from this transmission were *The Sacred Path of Love* and *The Sacred Path of Peace* with the high frequency of Mary Magdelene and Jeshua. There has been a continual upgrade in my capacity to receive these pure teachings through my sincere desire to be a vessel of truth with a willingness to return to being a child of my Divine heritage.

With this new work *Divine Soul Empowerment,* I have received the teachings that are most necessary at this time. The lower frequencies that have plagued this world are now being infused with the Light, thus allowing the corrective codes of Divine intelligence to be received; resulting in the dissolution of the deep patterns of separation and control by the egoic nature of the human condition. ▶

The transmission reveals that the body is the aspect of self-centeredness and when the "I am" identification is limited to "I am the body," "I am this," "I have this" and so forth, it creates a web around the field that keeps one in karma. The "I want" completed by "something" is the bondage that must be mastered to ascend to the clear light of being, which is simple presence. Simply allowing *what is to be* without a label, permits the "I" to be left at that and to rest in the heart without definition.

Broken Open By Grace is the state in which the "I" no longer needs a statement to be something. The "I" can rest in its own isness. The many lifetimes of striving, running from pain to pleasure and pleasure to pain, halt in the face of Grace.

Grace reveals the essence of being that has always been there. Nothing to attain or gain. In the very empty stance of being, Grace fills your chalice with immeasurable sense of knowing your Source, returning to the Father, returning to innocence; your child-like being.

The Wound is the place where
the Light enters you.

Rumi

The light enters consciousness when the heart breaks open from being trapped in the illusion of separation of the ego self. Consciousness raises through this increase in light as the body becomes a vehicle for this great blessing.

The identification with self, known as "body consciousness" is the core of self-centered being, the cause of great suffering. The ascension upward to know yourself as Divine begins to diffuse the belief in separation and the self-centered mechanisms become dysfunctional. When this happens, one must ask for help, ask for guidance so the energy can follow the new intention for awakening consciousness to meet its Source. When the soul is trapped in the karmic condition of identification there must be a sincere yearning to be free.

Reach for God

I welcome you to this work of *Divine Soul Empowerment* and hope you take precious moments of your day to receive these teachings of the Council of Light.

You are truly blessed with great Spiritual Light and Love.

With great humility and service,

Jaya Sarada

Seek and the door will open.

Rumi

About this book

*A sacred text that includes mandala coloring, journaling
and spiritual practices to support your life path.*

LIVING IN THE LIGHT

This section initiates the awareness that you are pure light. You are the
same light as God, the Divine presence that has created you. This light
is here to guide you on your life path.

DIVINE SOUL EMPOWERMENT SACRED GUIDANCE

This section offers you profound transmissions and guidance that will
assist you in opening your heart to the highest frequencies of life.

THE SACRED ORACLE

Gifts for your Soul - 11 Divine Soul Empowerments to nurture the
light in your daily life.

DIVINE SOUL CARE

A resource manual to assist you in vibrational care of your body,
mind and soul.

DIVINE SOUL MEDITATIONS

Begin or end your day with these powerful transmissions and
meditations that will clear and renew your precious being and offer
you a deep sense of peace for your life.

Introduction

*T*he Council of Light is here to tell you the purpose of their work.

Postponement of awakening is no longer an option for most souls. The earth frequencies are moving into the next dimension of Divine consciousness. Now is the time to free yourself from the bondage of ego consciousness which is the conditioning of mankind to believe in separation and fear. The time is urgent to become free of the old ways and evolve or ascend into the realm of being which is living in the world but not of it.

An invitation awaits you to take the steps needed so your soul can be fully empowered. Join with the circle of light in service to the evolution of awakening love for all of humanity. This message is the direct teaching of the masters for those who are ready to raise their vibration to a higher consciousness; one that holds the Divine principles of God.

Because of the density of the mental plane, it has become very difficult to receive the higher frequencies of the Divine. *Divine Soul Empowerment* is now a path to freedom and awakening. In this work, you will be guided to release the sense of your separate self and meet the unknown mystery of your being. You will be shown the doorways to open your heart to the highest frequency of your soul. Through this empowerment process you will be guided to let go of tendencies, patterns and ancestral conditioning that keep you from the ultimate happiness of your soul. Your soul will no longer choose that which is not working for you.

This work is encoded with ascension frequencies of the masters and by experiencing it you will be gifted with tools to uncover the light within.

The path of ascension brings to your life many levels of transformation. In each stage you will learn about Divine action; the embodiment of your soul's awakening. This action may be viewed as the innate intelligence of your soul that guides you to align with the eternal principles of the Divine.

Listen within to the calling of the masters...
*Your consciousness may move through the
following transcendent gateways:*

GATEWAY 1:

You see clearly the ancestral conditioning that has layered your being with misidentification. In service to awakening, you choose to change the core of your being to be aligned with the highest vibration. You affirm protection, well-being and freedom for your life.

GATEWAY 2:

You realize that deep inside you lives a Divine being. This Divine being is worthy of great love and respect. You choose to love yourself as a child of God.

GATEWAY 3:

You witness the play of the separate nature of the self and how it has strived for power and control. Through seeing and releasing the pattern of identification, you empower your Divine soul.

GATEWAY 4:

You listen inwardly from the deepest regions of your sacred heart. Here you will find the chalice of wisdom within that is accessed through your silent contemplation.

GATEWAY 5:

You endeavor to speak from your true essence rather than your ego nature. You understand you are a sacred being and that you have the power to create your life in alignment with your highest good. You receive your soul nourishment through silence.

GATEWAY 6:

You choose to see through the eyes of God, with the compassion of your open heart. You find peace when you turn toward your true nature.

GATEWAY 7:

You see that all aspects of your life are integrated with your Divine purpose of self-knowing. You practice surrender of the personal self and you embrace your soul as unified expression of God, embodiment of your truest essence.

The Ascension Way

- Be kind to all people. Through your kindness, you will enter the Kingdom.

- Trust in yourself as a dynamic energy being and allow yourself to be guided by the frequency of joy.

- Forgive all, for they know not what they do when veiled by the ego self.

- Love yourself as you love God. Love others as you love yourself.

- Through quiet meditation, cultivate your awareness of light, so you may attune yourself to Divine frequencies.

- Release the contents of your mind and open your heart to the infinite nature of love.

- Become as a child within your heart so you may share in the joy of the creator.

- You are the space in which all is appearing. Return to this space and allow life to happen.

- Your life is not merely birth and death. The intention of life is to empower your Divine soul. Let yourself hear the calling.

. . . the blessings are always there.

Darkness cannot drive out darkness; only light can do that.
Hate cannot drive out hate; only love can do that.

Martin Luther King Jr.

Section I

Living in the Light

You are the Light of the World

see my light within your sacred heart

This light is what perceives the truth.

Most minds are veiled by the identification of the self that has been created by thought. When the mind is quiet, then thoughts are quiet, allowing space for the true self to experience its Source of Divine consciousness. The more the self experiences the Source of being, the more light that is activated in the world. Seek the light of your inner being as you would seek your needs of survival.

The light of your inner being will be with you eternally, but the body is a temporary form that lives in the dimension of time. Wisdom is knowing the truth of this temporary form and turning toward the light of the infinite consciousness of God. Sorrow is a result of not knowing the truth of being. Welcome this life as a precious time to understand the nature of reality.

Gratitude leads us to view life as precious and to understand that life is continually nurturing us to our fullest potential. But the real investment of your life force is to devote your soul to the discovery of what is the eternal. This way of living brings true value. When a soul uncovers its true essence it is the highest form of love, a love that leads consciousness from the darkness to the light.

You Give Your Soul to God...
God Returns Profound Grace Upon Your Life

Meet your own self. Be your own self.
Listen to it, obey it, cherish it, keep it in mind ceaselessly.
You need no other guide.
As long as the urge for truth affects your daily life, all is well.

Nisargadatta Maharaj

With the light,
you will become a vessel of love.

With the light,
you will trust in your soul to guide you home.

With the light,
you will transcend the sorrow of the world.

Temple Time
Communion with Your Divine Source

ight is your true consciousness.

You must live within the vibration of light consciousness to be free and to know true joy. This is the living waters of truth within you. When you release attachment to the realm of the transitional earth life, you begin to live in the eternal. This eternal light is your Source of well-being. You will understand the nature of Divine law when you are no longer locked in the matrix of this earth dimension.

Begin by turning within to the light of your heart. Take a few deep breaths and allow your mind to soften. When you sink deep within your heart, you commune with God. This is your time of unity with your Source. Allow the experience of unity to illuminate areas of your life that need healing. Ask God to heal patterns, afflictions or wounds in your energy field. By communing with God you awaken the transformational power of your love. The healing force is infinite, unbound and carries you to the realm of the miraculous.

- Practice returning to the light often, so you may receive the wisdom of God.

- Rest in your sacred heart, so you may know the peace of God.

- Live your life in quiet surrender so you may know the grace of God.

Divine Soul Empowerment
living in the light

*M*any of us go through our whole life by living in the past.

We unconsciously allow our experiences to cloud the gift of the present moment. These experiences are known as the scars or Vasanas of our soul. But they are not our true nature because they are held in the past and in truth are non-existent. The ego is composed of all our past experiences and by filtering the present through the past, the ego stays in control. This bondage to the illusionary nature of life is what causes great suffering.

The work of *Divine Soul Empowerment* is to identify the Vasanas of our soul and through the feeling body instill a healing frequency that will release these scars from lifetimes of soul loss. This healing frequency is activated through surrender to God. When we surrender everything to our Source, we return to our true nature as a child of God and activate the original Holy teachings. Through fully embracing the present and releasing the past, we are freed from the lost thoughts of the ego and become vibrant with the activation of God's light. *Divine Soul Empowerment* is the moment of your rebirth and awakening, and the embodiment of the Divine blueprint of your soul.

Receive Your Divine Source of Power.

This is the path of Divine Soul Empowerment,
the release of separation from your Divine Source.

Above you is a Star of infinite light, beauty, power and love.
From this Star, the light is pouring upon you.
Attune yourself to this central point of power... it is your life.
White Eagle

Section II

Divine Soul Empowerment
Sacred Guidance

Vibrational Resonance with the Divine

Our beautiful soul's essence is created by God. This most Holy frequency is our natural frequency. But, because of our human psychology and conditioning, our minds have formed a separate sense of self as our true identity. In turn, we often accumulate vibrations that are not true to our real essence. This results in the experience of suffering. It is through deep surrender that our soul is revealed as a spark of the Divine, and radiantly expresses the light of joy.

Divine light is the Source that removes all separation and elevates our soul to the natural frequency of joy. Through our breath, we simply release the hold on the mind and allow our being to ascend to the higher frequencies of our soul's light.

Life is meant to be free...

Life is meant to live in joy...

Life is the expression of the Creator's love.

Light is Your Guide
to the Kingdom

Life is pure grace, a gift bestowed
upon you from God.
Through your breath you are brought
into form and through your breath
you are taken home.
This is your time of grace.
God's light is your guidance to
follow for your return to the Kingdom.
This Holy light is always with you.
You are this light.
You need nothing else
but to remember.

7 Keys to the Kingdom

These keys are stepping stones to the Kingdom.
As you embody these truths your inner light opens the door,
and leads you to the formless consciousness of your Divine nature.

- Leave everything behind and enter with your true and
  uncovered essence.

- Witness life on earth as a training ground for your awakening.

- Love your true nature without any sense of being something
  other than a child of God.

- Listen to your inner guidance to receive your assignment
  from Spirit. This assignment is the work of the Council of
  Light that will assist in alleviation of mankind's suffering on earth.

- Forgive everything that you have experienced in the earth
  dimension and raise your frequency out of the bondage of
  time, into the frequency of timeless love.

- Love the experiences of your life, as they are the fire that
  propels you to return to your Divine Source.

- Your Holy breath is the breath of Divine consciousness.
  Through your breath, you are able to release lifetimes of sorrowful
  memories. Through your breath you are able to receive the light
  needed to restore your soul to its highest potential.

Return to your breath.
What can you release today that is not serving your highest expression of light?
Write down what you can give back to God so you may heal.

Whoever brought me here will have to take me home.
Rumi

Unity Consciousness

To understand unity consciousness we must first understand that we are never separate from God. Our sense of separation stems from our mind and is born from thoughts and emotions. These thoughts and emotions create a web of identity and our patterns solidify this forged identity. We live our life according to our perceptions which are coming from experiences in the past or thoughts that are a projection of fear into the future. This is what creates the web of being. To release the thoughts and emotions that mask our true nature, it requires serious investigation or inquiry into the nature of thought.

So how do we begin?

We have been instilled with a most precious tool from the Divine: Love. So, the tool for this inquiry is love, and we have also been gifted with a sacred heart that is the keeper of this love. The sacred heart within each one of us is a vessel of the Holy Spirit, and has never been separate from our Divine Source.

To enter the sacred heart one must be willing to remove the veil and leave the separate sense of self behind. Spend time each day with the question *"Who Am I"* and through this inquiry the veils of false identity begin to fall away. There is a doorway to the sacred heart, but only an unadulterated being can enter. So, we must enter completely naked, we must enter unburdened. When we dive deeper into pure being, we will be welcomed into our sacred home with God. The Holy energy will purify the fragments of our self, and reunite our soul with our Source.

This is the path of healing and the
path of unity with our Divine soul.

The sacred heart within each one of us
is a vessel of the Holy Spirit.

When you step out of the haze there is nothing but
beauty, serenading your soul to its origin.

Love is Unity

Love is unity, love is letting go of the illness and sorrow of separation. With love, there can be no separation, as love is the essence of unity. When we see the fictitious ego-self for what it is, we are liberated from its grasp and return to our Divine being, one with God. When we allow the love of God to immerse our being in unity, we are freed from the unreal, and delivered to truth.

Let Go of Your Worries

Let go of your worries and rest in your
diamond like heart, like the face of a mirror that
contains no images. If you want a clear mirror,
behold yourself and see the shameless truth,
which the mirror reflects.

If metal can be polished to a mirror-like finish,
what polishing might the mirror of the heart
require? Between the mirror and the heart is this
single difference: the heart conceals secrets,
while the mirror does not.

Rumi

Explore the question Who Am I?
Beyond your title, status, physicality, story and ideas, who resides?

The sacred heart within each one of us is a vessel of the Holy spirit.

The Inner Temple

Within you lives the light of the Divine. This light is the aspect of your being that is unified with God. It is always present. For many of us, we have given our life over to the separate self, the story of "me." Our entire life is lived through this story, a composition of beliefs that we have adapted from perceptions, patterns and projections. Behind all thought and stories, lives the eternal presence of being that is simply still, listening, witnessing.

To find peace, turn within to your inner temple and invite the mind to rest. To enter your inner temple, you simply practice silence. It is through silence, you release the mechanism of thought and enter the experience of spiritual light.

The sorrow of misidentification is the human condition, one that has captivated souls for lifetimes. With God's grace you can learn to surrender the sorrow of the human condition and offer it all to the altar within your inner temple of light.

Your truth becomes activated from surrendering the false nature of self, and wisdom is born from this truth. Love is awakened within your heart and you become a witness to the light of your true nature.

The light of your inner temple shines upon your path, leading you home to the Kingdom. This light is in great service to the spiritual awakening of humanity.

Turn Within Toward Your Light

Your heart is your inner temple where you turn to receive sacred guidance.
Deep within your soul lives the essence of your true being.
This Holy temple within is the heart of God's creation.
The temple within your heart is also the temple within God's heart.
When you guide your mind to the stillness within,
you will receive the light of your being.

Spend some time in silent meditation.
Spend enough time that the world and your thoughts begin to fade away.
What do you sense in that space? What does silence teach you?

The mind creates the abyss, the heart crosses it.
Sri Nisargadatta Maharaj

Release the investment in thoughts.

Allow yourself to be enveloped in spiritual light.

Meet Your True Self

Open the door to your inner temple.

Take time each day to sit in silence.

Spend moments communing with nature.

Breathe deeply.

Practice forgiveness and letting go of the past.

Offer all sorrow to God.

Inquire into the nature of suffering.

Discover what is eternal within your being.

Live with great compassion and gentle kindness.

Your Soul's Essence

Your soul is the essence of your Divine being whose true home is within the realm of God. It is independent of form and is eternal in nature with all the attributes of the Divine. Even though you are only on this earth for a very short time, your soul is traveling through this dimension on the infinite path to your ever-unfolding potential.

It has now become urgent for each precious being to realize their soul is their true essence, not their mind and emotions. The emotional body of the soul is the condition of the patterns of thought within the mind. When the body dies, so does the emotional body. But impressions from emotions and thought patterns can be carried in the causal body, where the records of the soul are stored. These records must be released in order for the soul to be free. Soul loss is the result of living lifetime to lifetime, without knowing or realizing your purpose as a being of God. Reclaiming your true essence is the beginning of soul recovery.

We are here to embody our Divine being, and that makes it necessary for us to see and understand the cause of our suffering. When we transcend the human condition and the seeds of sorrow, we receive the wisdom to awaken and to serve our true purpose.

If you bring forth what is within you,

what you bring forth will save you.

If you do not bring forth what is within you,

what you do not bring forth will destroy you.

Gospel of Thomas

Although you appear in earthly form,
your essence is
pure Consciousness.
You are the fearless guardian of
Divine Light.

Rumi

Receive the Silent Essence
of Your Eternal Nature.

Transcendence of the lower realms is the task of your
soul's inner mastery. From lifetime to lifetime the body
rebirths the patterns of the ego, which results in the
continual experience of separation.

In each moment God is calling you to return home
to your timeless being. When you let go and fall into
God's embrace, the light of the Creator will transcend
all patterns of sorrow, setting you free.

Have there been hidden blessings in the hard areas of your life?
What have you learned from the challenges on your journey?

The consciousness in you and the consciousness in me,
apparently two, really one, seek unity and that is love.

Sri Nisargadatta Maharaj

Seek the Kingdom
the yearning of return

The journey to God can be difficult at times as you move through the changing landscape of joy and sorrow. The very fact that the body is a temporary vehicle, creates an urgency for you to discover what is real. Create time in your life to unveil the most valuable essence of your being; the boundless, everlasting light of your Soul. The sacred light within you will guide you home to the Kingdom. The beautiful path of return will be revealed as you become more deeply devoted to your Divine Source. God will guide you to uncover the Holy ways of your true nature, such as forgiveness, stillness, breath, acceptance, allowance and love. When you activate these facets of your energy, peace will become your abiding nature.

Life becomes a mystical journey when you begin to learn the levels of consciousness as well as the vibrational qualities of the Creator. When you become interested in the truth, you will be able to see what is real and discern what is temporal. Instead of being the status quo, another being that has fallen asleep, your journey will become one of ascension, evolving your consciousness to hold more and more light, expanding your energy into pure beingness.

Now is the time to hear the call of God.

The Light is Your Guide

*L*ight is your guide to the Kingdom of God. When you know light, you are on the path. When you can discern the difference between the vibration of darkness and the vibration of light, you will be able to make choices for your life that are in alignment with the Divine.

Many souls are not interested or willing to experience their own light. They are convinced their mind and all of its concepts are correct, and that they are in control.

The mind's vibration can never be pure though, because it obscures everything it sees and experiences through mental and emotional memory. When we give all of our power to our thoughts, we solidify those thoughts with emotions and we jump into the storm of a never-ending reaction to what is appearing in our life. We may also suppress the light that is trying to heal us, and we become numb to our own presence.

When there is light, there is joy, clarity and peace; this is your key to being able to intuit your highest good. If there is confusion or the sense of discordance, it is an indication to pause and to nurture your inner stillness. In silence the highest good will be revealed, on its own timing. Remember you are not in control, trust that God is guiding you.

To remove the discordance you must penetrate it with the light by diving into the eternal stillness, into the background of all movements of the mind.

This is the way to the Kingdom.

Trust in Love to Open the Door

High vibration is your birthright.
The lower vibrations of the man-made world
are obstacles on your journey for you to transcend
through love. The mind is the creator of the
illusion of the world. Your heart is the
creator of Heaven within you.

Seek the Kingdom before all else and your heart will
become a beacon of light on your passage home.

Listen to the Divine melody in your heart.
Take a few deep breaths and allow your mind to rest in your heart.
Receive the light within your heart and direct this
light to all the cells of your body.
Trust in light to bring harmony to your body, mind and spirit.
With wholly trust in God, you will experience a profound
rebirth of your soul's true essence.

Return to your breath...
Spend some time in your day following the frequency of joy and trusting in God.
Let go of any thoughts that create discordance in your energy.
What happens? What does life reveal?

When I die, I will send down a shower of roses from the Heavens,
I will spend my time in Heaven by doing good on earth.

St. Therese of Lisieux

Love is the Flowering of Grace

grace is the seed of infinite love

Throughout life there are many experiences of joy and sorrow. This is the nature of life in a body.

Take a moment to contemplate the impermanent nature of life.

Witness your life as a changing picture on the screen called life. See that throughout all changes there has always been a guiding force watching, protecting and guiding you in your life. As you witness your life, trust that you are also being witnessed and held by the hand of the Holy One taking you home.

Through letting go of the idea that you are a person who is in control of life, you naturally return to the innocence of being.

In this mystical authentic state there is sacred unity with your Source.

With daily practices you will live
as a light of the Divine and will become
a vessel for God's work.

Pointers of Grace:

Fall in love with God within you, love your self as God.

Grace is the light of God. This light lives as a Holy presence within your sacred heart.

Grace brings you the wisdom to transcend your karma so you can use the lessons of your soul as the priceless foundation for your awakening.

Grace is an ease of being, where you are free to be, free to soar into your infinite potential.

Grace is the simple but profound blessing of the present moment.

Grace is knowing the peace and love of your true essence.

Grace is the Power
of Transformation

Grace is the Divine calling to return you to your true nature. Through grace, your heart yearns for the Beloved. Without grace, you simply live life through the cyclical experience of birth, old age, sickness and death. The unknowing of who you really are is the sorrow of humanity.

But, you have a choice.

To choose to live in alignment with God is the inner work of your soul, which is grace. This alignment occurs when your energy turns from a linear pathway to a vertical, upward channel. Your life force moves up through your life channel embodying the grace of being.

Grace is the Divine Father,
the Divine Mother,
holding your hand on your journey home.

Return to your breath...
What do you practice to nurture your Divine being?
How do you invite grace into your life?

Grace is always present. You imagine it is something somewhere high in the sky, far away, and has to descend. It is really inside you, in your Heart, and the moment you effect subsidence or merger of the mind into its Source, grace rushes forth, sprouting as from a spring within you.

Ramana Maharshi

The Holy Passageway

the hidden chamber within your sacred heart

Time is the vehicle to evolve in love. The benevolent path to awakening resides deep with your sacred heart. Through your sincere yearning to realize your truest self, you begin the journey to the deepest region of your heart where you will receive the gifts of your soul's light.

Through lifetimes you have experienced many lessons that have revealed the nature of illusion and sorrow. These tests have been necessary for your soul to see the truth.

With your breath, release the sorrow of your life...
With your breath receive the light of the Divine...
With your breath, become one with God.

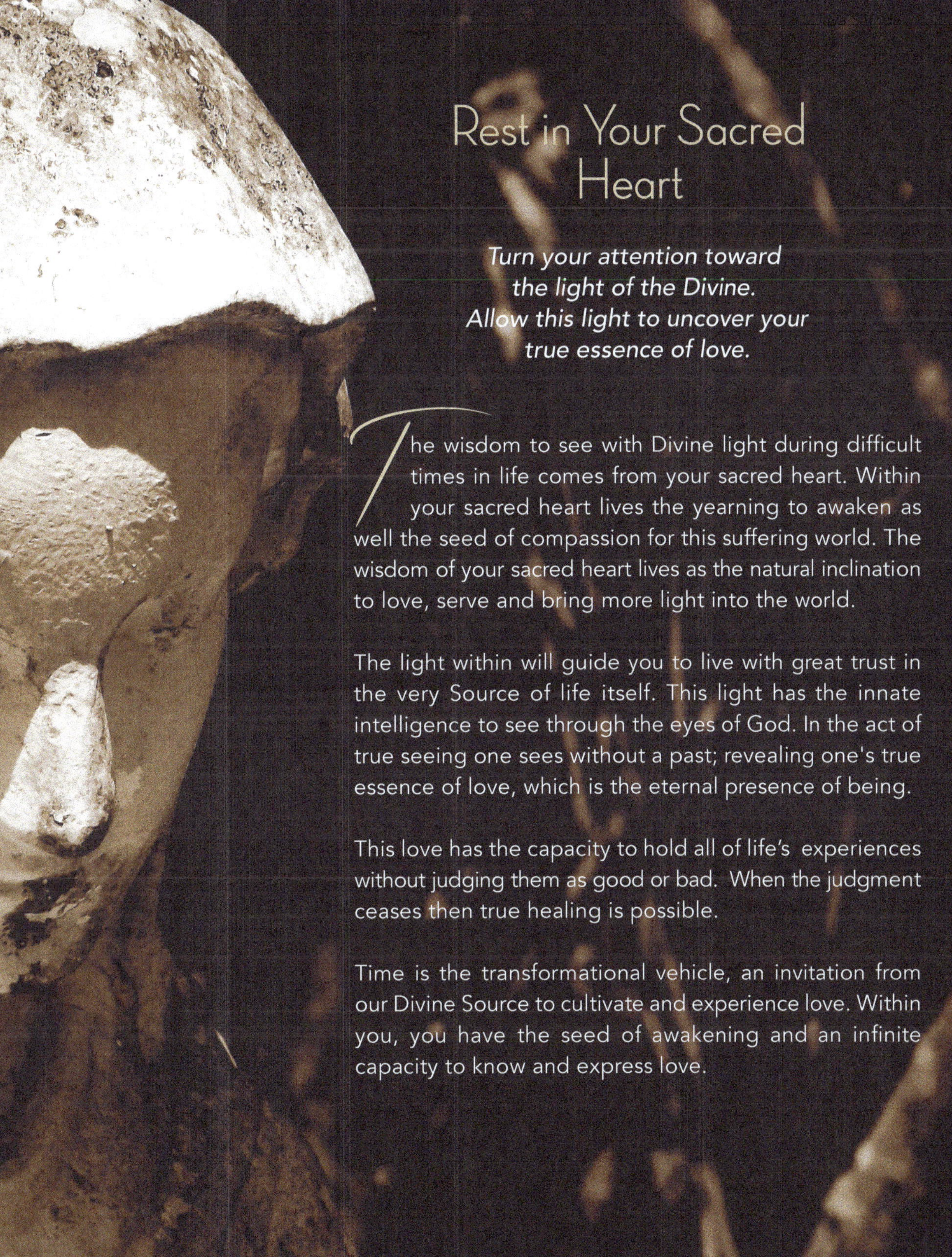

Rest in Your Sacred Heart

*Turn your attention toward
the light of the Divine.
Allow this light to uncover your
true essence of love.*

The wisdom to see with Divine light during difficult times in life comes from your sacred heart. Within your sacred heart lives the yearning to awaken as well the seed of compassion for this suffering world. The wisdom of your sacred heart lives as the natural inclination to love, serve and bring more light into the world.

The light within will guide you to live with great trust in the very Source of life itself. This light has the innate intelligence to see through the eyes of God. In the act of true seeing one sees without a past; revealing one's true essence of love, which is the eternal presence of being.

This love has the capacity to hold all of life's experiences without judging them as good or bad. When the judgment ceases then true healing is possible.

Time is the transformational vehicle, an invitation from our Divine Source to cultivate and experience love. Within you, you have the seed of awakening and an infinite capacity to know and express love.

Within Your Heart Lives the Peace of God

Within your heart lives the peace of God. This is your true home. To know this peace is to rest within your sacred heart. The mind, when directed to the silent cavern of your heart, will naturally rest. This is the path to true being. Within the Kingdom there are many souls who have dissolved the prison of the mind. When you unify in the consciousness of God, you will receive your birthright of everlasting peace.

It is always the false that makes you suffer, the false desires and fears, the false values and ideas, the false relationships between people. Abandon the false and you are free of pain; truth makes happy, truth liberates.

Sri Nisargadatta Maharaj

Peace is your natural state...
Peace is the highest vibration of God...
Peace is freedom from sorrow.
Peace be with you.

In what ways can you practice compassion?
How does compassion integrate with forgiveness?

The heart is a thousand-stringed instrument that can only be tuned with Love.

Hafiz

The Path of Ascension
toward a higher vibration

This life is a path of ascension toward your Divine soul. Each time you turn toward the light of God, you move upward in your vibration and you meet a new aspect of your true nature.

Time is the measurement of your life in a body, but cannot define your eternal being. Your journey is timeless, and the doors will mystically open to the light of your being.

The path of ascension is a journey of self realization. You will experience soul tests as you evolve in your wisdom. This wisdom expands from your heart and becomes the force of your soul's ascension. Each being has a limitless capacity to hold more love and infinite potential to express their Divine essence.

Put your thoughts to sleep,
do not let them cast a
shadow over the moon
of your heart.

Let go of thinking.

Rumi

Awakening Your Light Body

To awaken your inner light body is to let go of all the contents of form and receive the formless light of the Divine. Your light body is the vehicle that has been created for you to travel through infinity.

When you let go of the content of the mind, the vibration of your Source remains. The eternal light can never be removed or diminished as it is all there is. Become like a chalice of the light, receive the light and allow it to purify the mind. Within your chalice, Source remains. This most sacred light will heal the wounds of separation that are stored in your karmic body by opening your heart to unconditional Love.

This light is your key to the Kingdom.

Jaya Sarada

If you knew yourself for even one moment,
if you could just glimpse your most beautiful face,
maybe you wouldn't slumber so deeply
in that house of clay.

Why not move into your house of joy
and shine into every crevice!
For you are the secret Treasure-bearer,
and always have been.
Didn't you know?
Rumi

Return to your breath...
How do you invoke the light on a daily basis?
What can you do to cultivate more light in your life?

Wrapped up in Yourself, you hid from me.
All day I looked for you and when I found you hiding inside me.
I ran wild, playing now me, now You.

Lalla

Transcendence

healing the emotional body

Our ego forms judgments about our experiences and these judgments often hold the frequencies of shame and guilt. These frequencies are programs created by our ego. And we engage in these programs whenever we believe in our ego as a separate entity from God. These frequencies are not unique to each individual, they are held in collective consciousness, and each time they are activated they strengthen the sorrow of humanity.

Shame, the product of the separate nature of the self who feels badly about itself, is a powerful pointer toward God. It is simply a reminder that all acts of separation create the lower emotions of shame, guilt, fear, etc. It is also an indication to surrender to your Divine Source and allow God to heal you. When we engage in harmful programs, all we have to do is to ask God to release us, and to return us to unity.

When you begin this practice of returning, no matter what has occurred, you increase your personal capacity for light and you evolve Divine consciousness.

This inner work requires observation of the separate sense of self and the ability to allow Divine love to heal the emotional body.

To heal the emotional body you must be willing to let go of the past with
the many emotional judgments held from unhealed experiences.
Simply let go and allow your true essence to
emerge in the present moment.

To be free is to let go.

To really heal is to know God,
to see God, and to do the work of God.

Nurture your true essence as a light on this planet.
No matter your circumstance, surrender all fear, and
trust in your Source which has never left you.
When you seek the Kingdom before all else,
you will know God.

Even when tied
in a thousand knots,
the string is still but one.
Rumi

elcome the ego self or separate nature of self with great love and compassion and see it holds the wounds of separation, both individually and in humanity. This aspect of self exists in patterns of survival and has been necessary to a point for your soul's growth. For most of life many of us exist primarily through the patterns of our ego, its reactions and traumas which have held us captive since very young. The mechanism of mind is useful in the world only when it is in service to the heart, when it is surrendered to God.

When we embrace the ego for what is, instead of shaming it or allowing it to intoxicate us, it softens and begins to release its grasp. In order to return to unity and wholeness, it is essential we allow the fragmented parts of our consciousness to be seen. Instead of firming the division of thought through right and wrong, we must let go of what does not really exist and become steadfast as beings of peace and pure presence. It is the witnessing of the ego and the disengagement from its importance that liberates our consciousness.

Purely by spending time investigating what is eternal and what is unchangeable we strengthen our God Self, and guide the ego to be in its intended place: to naturally rest in the heart. There is a visible energetic alignment in those who have put God before all else, in those who understand they are simply children of God.

Return to your breath...
What does seek the Kingdom before all else mean to you?
How can you apply this in your daily life?

Love says, "I am everything." Wisdom says, "I am nothing."
Between the two, my life flows.

Sri Nisargadatta Maharaj, I Am That

Your Soul's Freedom

Your personal self is on a journey to evolve and unify with the highest aspect of your being, which is your soul. Your soul is your eternal essence that has the work of healing separation from your Divine Source.

Your soul is from the highest dimension of God, and is untouched, formless and free from identification with changing personality. Your soul is simply a witness of this manifested world. See now, there is something within you that is free from time, free from thought and emotions, free from memory, free from identity. Your soul is the light of God and is untouched by all the sorrows of life.

The damage that is experienced through being in form, identifying with the personal self, doing harm to oneself and others, lives in the dimension of time.

The scars that have occurred from being in a body, from lifetime to lifetime, exist in the records of the soul, to be healed by God. These are the akashic records of your soul, but do not affect the purity of your soul.

Observing the beauty of nature, we learn to understand the purest essence of creation, as nature has no thought of who it is. Nature simply is the beauty of God's creation. In your truest reality, you are the essence of nature, a seed of life that moves through infinity, awakening your true potential as a being of light. Your essence is expressing on earth in form, but it is a temporary stop-over on your eternal journey of expansion

Presence of being is your highest expression in freedom.
In presence there is only God and in God there is only love.

The Freedom to Soar

Your light is your wings to freedom.
This light only knows freedom.
When this light is veiled by
the human condition there is
restriction and bondage.
Freedom is your birthright.
It is available to all who wish to
soar into their Divine potential.
Freedom is received by letting go.

This is love:
To fly toward a secret sky, to cause a hundred veils to fall each moment.
First, to let go of life.
In the end, to take a step without feet;
to regard this world as invisible, and to disregard what appears to be the self.
Heart, I said, what a gift it has been to enter this circle of lovers,
to see beyond seeing itself, to reach and feel within the breast.

Rumi

Our journey is to understand the purest essence of creation.

Return to your breath...
What patterns can you release so your soul may be liberated.
How would you live if you knew you were free?

The mind creates the abyss, the heart crosses it.

Nisargadatta Maharaj

Love is the Truth of Your Soul

To forgive is to know that the ego-self is blinded by fear. This fear is rooted in the conditioned thought of being separated from God. Seeing that the mind has formed a separate sense of self and lives to uphold its identity is the first step in freedom from the mind. Objective seeing is the seed of understanding the mind and its strategies for survival to maintain a separate sense of self. This understanding blossoms into love, the frequency of God. Allow this understanding to guide you home to the Kingdom.

Witness the mind of mankind, and how it operates under fear of attack; becoming the Source of great violence. Fear is the vibration that causes much pain to others. Millions of souls have lost their light due to the mind's creation of a separate sense of self. The test of this life is to see the mind and its child of sorrow and meet it face-on as the illusionary force that keeps you from love, your true essence.

Many people are suffering from the karma that has been created in the world because of our passive allowance of the conditioning of our consciousness. We contribute to this karma when we succumb to staying asleep in the illusion. The light is the powerful Source behind the mind-made reality. It is capable of instilling its healing force into the mental conditioning of all souls who ask.

Ask and you shall receive ...
Seek the Kingdom and you will be guided home.

The most urgent step for souls who wish to ascend into the
light of being is to decide to compassionately let go and forgive the past.
To begin now, find the light within your heart, in this very moment.
You only need to turn toward this Holy light and allow it to carry you home.

The Miracle of the Divine

Within you lives the miracle of the Divine; the wisdom to transform personal love into Divine love, the way of true forgiveness. This miracle offers you the strength to uplift love that is conditional and controlling, into love that is allowing and accepting. A love that has the wisdom to understand that all errors of our humanity stem from false identification.

 It is when there is a separate sense of self who is damaged by the story of the ego that conflict and division is born. When the separate nature of the self releases its hold, you ascend into a Divine realm where the wounds of the ego-self become healed.

In the Divine realm all is forgiven.

What was seen as the story of great sorrow caused by ignorance of your true nature is now viewed as the grace that is guiding you home. Through this grace, you will receive a renewed heart free from the pain of the past.

Through surrender your life is reborn.

A quiet mind is all you need. All else will happen rightly, once your mind is quiet. As the sun rises making the world active, so does self-awareness, affecting changes in the mind. In the light of calm and steady self-awareness, inner energies wake up and work miracles without any effort on your part.

Nisargadatta Maharaj

Return to your breath...
Your life is guided for you to reach your highest soul's potential.
In your witnessing what do you experience?

*Your task is not to seek for love, but merely to seek
and find all the barriers within yourself that you have built against it.*

Rumi

Remember the Light Within

fall back to your true nature

The seeing of the illusion of life is the first step in awakening. One must see with an empty mind, so that what is seen, is the naked truth without the veil of the mind. See the transient world of change that is appearing according to the ego's projection. This projection is the root cause of sorrow. Most humans are mixing the egoic projection with the pure essence of life.

The world is a playground for the mind. The sorrow of the soul is due to mind forming a separate self, burying your true self in its projections. The wisdom to see the truth is the precious light that is flowering in your being. This is witnessed by detaching your mind from what is untrue and temporary, while turning inward to the mysterious light of your own being which cannot be known by the mind.

Most sentient beings look to find themselves in the mental realm. When in truth, your soul is formless, boundless and can only be understood in the mystical silence of your true nature.

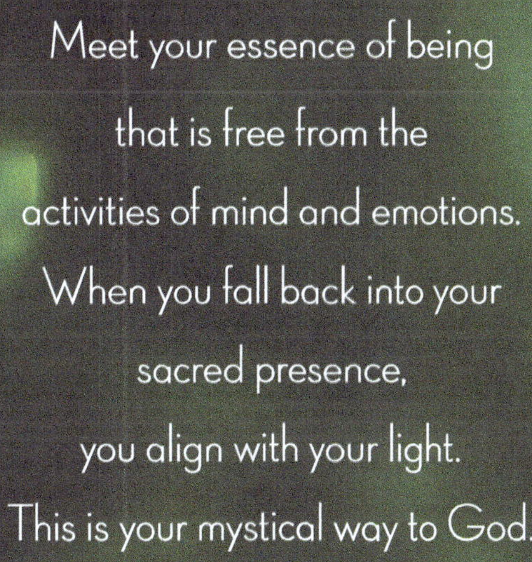

Meet your essence of being

that is free from the

activities of mind and emotions.

When you fall back into your

sacred presence,

you align with your light.

This is your mystical way to God.

If you look too closely at the form,
you miss the Essence.
Rumi

Joy is the expression of love when
you are unified with your truth.

The Love of Awareness

When you are in the vibration of love, you are naturally aware. In your presence, you love through your awakened heart. To access this love, take a deep breath and journey into the deeper region of your heart. This love is beyond personal love, it is the eternal love and ever-evolving love of your soul.

Love is the reason for your life.

Return to your breath...
allow your mind to return to the light of your heart.
This light is your highest intelligence. What is revealed?

All the darkness in the world cannot extinguish the light of a single candle.

St. Francis of Assisi

The Joy of Being

*remember when you felt
joy as your natural state?*

We are beings of dynamic energy. Energy that is either aligned with God or has succumbed to habitual patterns of fear. When we are able to clear our energy, and our mind is able to surrender its programs, there is a natural joy, a feeling of perfect peace and harmony no matter what is occurring. We return to the eternal state that is free.

Return to Joy
through guiding
the mind to rest in your heart.

Return to Joy
through quiet contemplation
on the true meaning of life.

Return to Joy
through communion with nature.

Remember Who You Are

Lifetimes have been lived in forgetfulness of your true essence. In each lifetime there are many experiences that are held in the records of your soul. The accumulation of these experiences are what clouds our being and makes us forget our light. We are not intended to live as burdened souls, we are intended to live as channels, as clear containers for God's will.

The mind is a mechanism of separation and seeks to create an ego identity apart from your Divine Source. This disconnection from Source has created the sorrow of mankind. Until there is a deep yearning for return to pure consciousness that is one with Source, the mind will continue to dominate your being.

The return to your true nature requires a willingness to release memory that is bound in time to pleasure and pain. This release of memory will free your soul to live as a being that is sovereign, light and living in potential. As you return to your true nature, your essence will appear as an innocent child of God.

When you feel a peaceful joy,
that's when you are near truth.

Rumi

Return to Innocence

When the ego releases its hold on your inner being, you naturally feel like you're floating as a balloon into the unknown, wonderous realm of life. This is the state of true innocence and joy. In this Divine realm all is forgiven since what is seen is the story of great sorrow caused by ignorance of your true self.

The grace of God will offer you a renewed heart that is free from the scars of memory. Through your willingness to let go and return to the innocence of being, you will return to your natural state of joy.

With joy there is innocence.

With joy there is light.

With joy there is love.

Become conscious of being conscious.
Say or think "I am",
and add nothing to it.
Be aware of the stillness that
follows the "I am".
Sense your presence,
the naked unveiled, unclothed beingness.
It is untouched by young or old,
rich or poor, good or bad,
or any other attributes.
It is the spacious womb of all creation,
all form.

Ramana Maharshi

Return to your breath...
see that your inner child has always been present, free, and in joy.
How would you feel if you lived from this state of innocence again?

Dance, when you're broken open. Dance, if you've torn the bandage off.
Dance in the middle of the fighting. Dance in your blood.
Dance when you're perfectly free.

Rumi

Presence of Being

Receive the gifts of your soul through falling back into your sacred heart. This is the spiritual practice necessary to release you from identification with the transitory nature of life.

Within you is a flow of Divine grace; take time each day to be with this sacred essence of your soul. This practice will guide you to healing the outer nature of life through invoking the healing light of your being.

Through your practice; breathe deeply as if you were sinking into the true essence of your soul.

Through your practice; dissolve the history that is held within the cells of your body so that you may breathe the fresh air of Spirit.

Through your practice; seek the Kingdom, your home of true and abiding peace.

In silence you meet the truth of your being.

In silence you transcend the lower emotions
and thoughts that keep you bound to suffering.

In silence you dissolve the personal nature of the self.

Silence: the Doorway to the Self

The inner realm of silence is your home of peace, where you turn to rest the mind and the mechanism of thought. This is the most important activity of your soul. As the body seeks nourishment for survival, your soul also needs silence to cultivate the eternal being within you. On each upward state of evolution, silence will be the foundation for your awakening.

A seeker of Truth looks beyond the apparent
and contemplates the hidden.

Rumi

The Song of Your Soul

Each soul is unique. Each soul is the authentic expression of God, and by embodying your soul's potential, you bring harmony and peace to the world.

Just as nature effortlessly operates in perfect balance, your essence when realized, gifts the world with the healing it needs.

No matter where you currently are in your life, there is a living sacred intention for your life, *The Song of Your Soul.*

Now is the time to embrace and express your essence as the awakened seed of God. Life and God are one.

Song of Life

J Krishnamurti

I have no name,
I am as the fresh breeze of the mountains.
I have no shelter;
I am as the wandering waters.
I have no sanctuary, like the dark gods;
Nor am I in the shadow of deep temples.
I have no sacred books;
Nor am I well-seasoned in tradition.
I am not in the incense
Mounting on the high altars,
Nor in the pomp of ceremonies.
I am neither in the graven image,
Nor in the rich chant of a melodious voice.
I am not bound by theories,
Nor corrupted by beliefs.
I am not held in the bondage of religions,
Nor in the pious agony of their priests.
I am not entrapped by philosophies,
Nor held in the power of their sects.
I am neither low nor high,
I am the worshipper and the worshipped.
I am free.
My song is the song of the river
Calling for the open seas,
Wandering, wandering,
I am Life.
I have no name,
I am as the fresh breeze of the mountains.

Return to your breath...
What brings you joy? What inspires you?
How do you tune in to the Divine intention for your life?

When you do things from your soul, you feel a river moving in you, a joy.

Rumi

Sacred Embodiment

your soul's purpose

The body is a great blessing; a vehicle for this earth school. And within the earth school, we have been given periods of time; themes of our soul and ancient stories to heal. Because we have been circling around the wheel of life and death, we may feel we have come to the end. We may feel exhausted from this karmic cycle.

The one thing that is true and non-changing is the ever evolving love within our hearts. This love is the reason for birth, the reason for death and is the eternal bond that propels us forward to create more and more capacity to hold more love.

Soul loss is the result of living lifetime to lifetime,
without knowing or realizing the purpose of your soul.

The Guidance to Recover Soul Loss

- Begin by realizing you're not your body or the conditioning that is inherent to human form.

- Invoke the essence of your soul within your heart.

- With your breath release your thoughts and guide your consciousness to your heart.

- Sense the peace of your true essence within.

- Ask God to soften your mind and awaken the light in your heart.

- By devoting your life to the transcendence of the sorrow of your ego and the world, you serve all of humanity.

Calling Yourself Home
remember who you are

When your ego surrenders and your soul awakens you will hear the call that is guiding you home. Through devoting yourself to stillness, to the place beyond the mind, you are born and become filled with life. The spacious vast mystery within you will release you from the lower dimensional energies so that you will travel in the sphere of God.

Know and see that you are the greatness of life itself, you are the Kingdom to which you are returning, you will never be alone, and you will never be in fear. You will embrace your birthright as a channel of the Divine and love will become your eternal home.

We are the Council of Light.

Return to your breath...

When you are at home in your sacred heart, how do you feel?

*We have been called to heal wounds, to unite what has fallen apart,
and to bring home those who have lost their way.*

St. Francis of Assisi

The Sacred Oracle

Gifts for Your Soul

Your guide to receive Divine messages to awaken
and align you with your highest soul's potential.

The Eleven Divine Soul Empowerments

Grace • Trust • Love • Light •

Compassion • Beauty • Courage

Joy • Unity • Wisdom

Devotion

I

The Gift of Divine Grace

I allow God's grace to envelop my heart

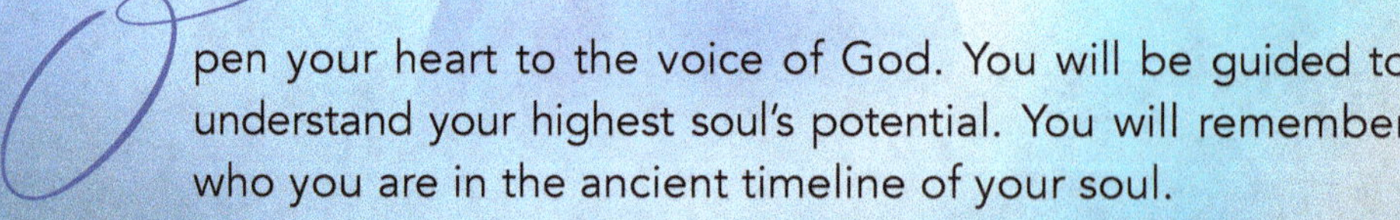

Open your heart to the voice of God. You will be guided to understand your highest soul's potential. You will remember who you are in the ancient timeline of your soul.

The Gift of Grace is with you as the beauty and light that nurtures your soul. Trust in grace to unfold the beautiful lotus of your heart. See grace in every moment and allow Divine grace to flow through you. When you trust in God, all answers are revealed.

I allow God's grace to freely flow through me
and guide me on my journey.

My life is an expression of grace leading me towards my soul's
awakening. I receive grace as the very breath I breathe.

II

The Gift of Divine Trust

Trust in the source of consciousness

You may feel lost on your journey at times and experience the weight of the dark night of the soul. In order to unite with the light, you must first experience what you are not, and see the illusion clearly. Instead of closing in and fixating on this constrained space, become aware of that which is always present. Feel the essence of life itself, existing within and without the parody of the lower self.

In this moment now you are pure consciousness, the beautiful container in which all of life appears. In all states, trust in the life-giving Source of your being and trust the light to illuminate your path home. With your breath let go, and allow the energy of the Divine to carry you.

I trust in my Source to light my path home.

I trust in myself to see this sacred light.

III

The Gift of Divine Love

To be truly empowered is to love yourself

as a child of God

Love is the essence of life. It lives as the force of nature in the mountains, flowers, trees and oceans. It is the light of every cell of the human body. Love is the breath of God. This is the highest understanding of love that a human being can know.

I open my heart to receive love.

I let go of all that keeps me from receiving
and giving Divine love.

I offer this love in service to God and to the
alleviation of the suffering of mankind.

IV

The Gift of Divine Light

There is nothing else but the light of the Divine

Divine light is the essence of your being. Your light will naturally shine when you release your grasp on your thoughts and emotions.

Nature is at one with God and when we spend time in nature it heals our mind. Feel the effortless being of the trees, the mountain, the wind, the sea. See how the miracle is beyond any thought. You are an extension of the same Source that pulls the tide. Let nature invoke your soul into harmony. Through your unity with your Divine Source, you become a beacon of light that is in service to the awakening of all beings.

The light of God lives within my heart and
through this sacred light I am carried home.

I seek the light within my heart
and offer this light to God.

V

The Gift of Divine Compassion

Compassion is the way of the unified soul

Compassion is the blossom of the strength of your true nature that will dissolve all sense of a separation. Compassion is the willingness to see that suffering in one's life is often due to misidentification of your truest essence with your ego self.

The experience of suffering is universal. When you understand the human condition, and know that you are one with all of life, compassion becomes the natural expression towards your self and others.

Receive the Gift of Compassion through letting go of the story of the separate nature of the self. Allow your heart to feel one with all beings and through knowing this oneness, compassion is born.

Within my heart lives the sacred essence of compassion.

Through compassion I offer a helping hand to others.

You may call God love, you may call God goodness.

But the best name for God is compassion.

VI

The Gift of Divine Beauty

The heart of God is the beauty of your soul

Beauty is the highest expression of truth that lives within your soul's essence. Beauty is your natural state, for in truth you are one with all of nature. When you allow yourself to receive life and to express life's miraculous and creative energy, there is beauty in everything you do.

By stepping out of the way, light is able to flow through you freely and beauty becomes the fullness of the present moment.

Beauty is the light of my being that lives
within my sacred heart.

I receive the beauty of God and allow
this beauty to flow through me.

I turn within to access the courage
needed for life's changes.

VII

The Gift of Divine Courage

The courage to return to light

The realization that you are an eternal being within a temporary body requires great courage. In a world that is fixated on the temporal, we are not taught to discover what is real. Sink into the presence that observes all and discover the stateless state. When you turn toward the light, and step beyond fear, a courage is uncovered within you that leads you home.

As a Divine being I am filled
with the strength of God.

VIII

The Gift of Divine Joy

Joy is the realization of eternal love

The gift of joy is your Divine birthright. To receive this joy, you simply need to allow it to dance in your heart. Joy is always here now when you relax into the present moment. Release all fears and feel the vibrating energy of life, the joy that expresses through your true nature.

Joy is the expression of God within your heart...
Joy is the light within your heart sharing its song with others...
Joy is your natural childlike nature, when thoughts are at rest.

Within my heart of light lives a wellspring of joy
that flows freely through my innocence.

When I become fully present in the moment
I feel the joy of this magical life.

IX

The Gift of Divine Unity

Unity is the place beyond fear

Turn within and you will feel your deepest self which is whole and unified with your Source. See that the only thing that takes you out of your natural state of unity is thought.

When you spend a few minutes each day in silence. You will nurture the unchanging aspect of your being. In this consciousness, you receive the Gift of Divine Unity.

I receive the Gift of Unity through simply being.

Through my surrender to the Divine

I am unified with God.

X

The Gift of Divine Wisdom

Love reveals light, light reveals wisdom

Wisdom blossoms through the light of your consciousness when unified with the love of your heart. See life as God sees life, with unconditional love and heartfelt awareness. Observe all of creation from the eternal heart and receive the Gift of Divine wisdom.

I receive the Gift of Divine Wisdom through resting my mind in my sacred heart.

I let go of my mind's movements and allow the wisdom
of God's light to embrace me.

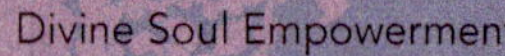

XI

The Gift of Divine Devotion

Devotion to my true nature leads me home

Your sacred heart is your true home. When you live from this place you naturally live with truth and great devotion to your Divine Source. Spend quiet moments and allow your being to journey deep into the cavern of your heart.

Within this sacred realm you experience letting go of any separation from God. Through surrender you deepen your spiritual devotion; through devotion you receive eternal peace.

I awaken the devotion of my heart to the

discovery of my true nature.

God is devoted to me as an
expression of his light,
I am devoted to God as
a chalice of his love.

When you are inspired by some great purpose,
some extraordinary project, all your thoughts break their
bonds; your mind transcends limitations;
your consciousness expands in every direction;
and you find yourself in a great,
new and wonderful world.

Patanjali

Section III

Divine Soul Care

raising your frequency from limitation to expansion

Awakening the Light Within

The Art of Energy Balancing

The Etheric Energy Field – Keys to Abundant Energy

Keys to Emotional Well-Being

Keys to Mental Well-Being

The Web of Mind & Emotions

The Emotional Field

The Temple of Your Soul-Your Akashic Light

Divine Breathing

The Chakras

- The soul is a living entity.
- The soul pervades the entire body.
- For the soul, there is neither birth nor death at any time.
- The soul has no past, present or future.
- The soul is indestructible, unbreakable and insoluble.
- The soul is unchangeable, immovable and eternally the same.
- The soul is invisible, inconceivable and immeasurable.
- The soul accepts new bodies, giving up old ones, just like a person puts on new garments, giving up old ones.

BhagavadGita ॐ

These bodies are perishable, but the dwellers in these bodies
are eternal, indestructible and impenetrable.

BhagavadGita ॐ

Awakening the Light Within
Your Luminous Aura - The Light Body

Everything is energy. We are energy beings that brings in and discharges energy in the great recycling system called life. Our energy flows as part of the natural process of life, from observing nature and learning from her rhythms; nature teaches us how to release, how to die, how to be reborn, how to blossom in beauty and how to let go again. It teaches us about stillness, movement, energy, light, dark, cold and hot. It teaches us about fire, wind, earth and water. These elements all reside in our body and express themselves energetically. Nature always leads us back to a feeling of equilibrium and calm. Because we are energy beings, we have the opportunity to see with our sixth sense and trust our Inner vision. We can also learn to see where we need energy protection and to ward off negative forces.

Our delicate etheric energies need protection from illness producing forces. Though in time, we are all subject to the simple processes of life, we can become the caretaker of our souls and work with our energy fields to create harmony, peace, good will and service in this lifetime. Saying "yes" to life means saying "yes" to good health, to positive thoughts and positive emotions. Saying "yes" means eliminating fear and negative thinking from our energy fields. We all have access to a great method to attain energy wellness, the Source of all healing. The Source is accessed through our willingness to receive our prayers, our breath, and great humility. Breathing healing light into our energy fields opens the path to the miracle of life itself. This Source, when consciously applied to any area of imbalance, brings us the miracle of healing.

I choose to keep my light body strong.

The Art of
Energy Balancing

A current of electromagnetic energy travels through our body, mind and spirit, giving us our life direction, life essence and life vitality. When energy is in balance there is a free flow of our life essence.

Each energy field functions optimally at a balanced frequency, an energy equilibrium. With energy balanced in the etheric, emotional, mental and spiritual energy fields, health follows. The frequency at which we resonate depends upon how we function on the etheric, emotional, mental and spiritual fields.

Watch for all that beauty reflecting from you
and sing a love song to your existence.

Rumi

*I choose to pay attention to my energy and
correct imbalances as they arise.*

The Etheric Energy Field – Keys to Abundant Energy

The etheric blueprint duplicates the physical body and when weakened shows signs of stress. Etheric energy imbalances are a result of stress on some level; when ignoring warning signs such as fatigue, loss of energy, depression and pain. When we listen to the body we can detect imbalances before they manifest as illness. We can learn to sense our internal messages and follow what the body is requiring for its sustenance. When the body speaks to us in the form of pain or discomfort, we become its most cherished caretaker. Honoring its messages and yielding to its direction brings balance to all aspects of our being. Through this listening we learn to apply the healing force of love to our life, observing the root cause of the imbalance.

For this, we must be honest about our thinking habits, our emotional expressions and our connection with nature and the Divine in life. If we are diligent, we can usually trace a physical symptom back to an emotional experience or a time of negative thinking. We can also observe when life is calling for communion with nature and the silence of our Divine self.

Our life essence enters through the chakras, and then flows into the nadis and meridians, nourishing the energy fields. Since the etheric energy is the blueprint of the physical, it is important to keep it strong and free from disturbances and energy blocks.

The etheric field is a bridge that relays information from the emotional and mental fields to the physical. Any emotional disturbance is very likely to impose some level of stress or pain on the body. If there is continual unresolved emotional or mental field disturbance it can eventually create disease in the physical body. The universal energy functions as life breath, or prana, and is received and distributed through the body. When prana is distributed freely throughout the etheric and released freely, the energy fields stay in harmony and balance.

I choose to restore my life force as needed.

Keys to Emotional Well-Being

In the emotional field, imbalances usually begin during periods of emotional stress when we are not allowing emotions to flow through and out of the body. When anger, for example, is suppressed time and time again, it often turns into depression, which can lead to a weakened system. On the other hand, continuous expression of strong anger can break down the internal organs and open the body to disease and disharmony. Healthy anger is merely a call to speak our truth at the appropriate moment with ease and honesty, but anger that is rooted in fear is a reflection of our disharmony with Divine energies. Transcend this kind of anger by increasing the vibration of love.

Emotions are a gift to understand others and ourselves. From them, we learn the art of listening to the voice of the heart. This requires energy and freedom from past emotions that color our experience of life in the now. When emotions accumulate from the past they become lodged in the aura, waiting for new experiences to assist in their release. Because of these past emotions it becomes difficult to live in the now.

To be well emotionally we must learn to let go, die to the past and release all past trauma. This means we must consciously surrender our attachment to memory, give all to the sacred fire of life and begin to fully live in the present.

*I choose to release the past and affirm
each new day with grace.*

Keys to Mental Well-Being

In the mental field, imbalances begin when the mind is not used constructively. The mind is like a piece of clay and needs to be molded and refined to become the most useful tool. When the mind is not directed properly, it is open to negative thinking habits that can result in illness and disharmony. The mind, when quiet, can be an instrument of beauty, perceiving spiritual truths of the universe. Through the quiet mind we have access to our higher nature, which holds the healing light of love, wisdom and compassion. The mind, when allowed to run unguided, expresses thoughts of a lower nature, directing the emotional level to anger, greed, desire, attachment, fear, envy and so forth.

When the mind is used as a witnessing tool, it is of great service on our journey, assisting us to stay centered, still and balanced through life's changes. When the mind is mastered, unwanted thoughts no longer dictate our actions and the attention turns from outward things back to the silence of the heart.

*I choose peace to be the foundation of my mind
and return to peace as needed.*

The Web of Mind & Emotions

The inner energy fields of the etheric, emotional, mental and spiritual bodies radiate out in the aura like a spectrum of rainbow light. When the energy is free from disturbances, the aura is luminous with light, beauty and aspiration. The school of life brings many tests and lessons so that you can grow into your full potential as a light being. Awakening to your true potential invites you to let go of areas in your life that hold a false sense of self through misidentification. You realize that you are not just your body, mind and emotions, and begin the search for deeper answers as to the nature of your true self.

Your emotions and thoughts influence your energy frequency. When you feel and think in ways that support your health and well-being, your energy frequency vibrates at a higher level. When you feel and think in ways that are not supportive to your health and well-being, your frequency is at a lower level. The conscious raising of your vibration serves to maintain your health on all levels.

In Eastern teachings, Kama-Manasic is the word used to describe the web of mind and emotions. When there are unresolved emotional and mental patterns, it becomes frozen energy in the field, creating a web that is often difficult to overcome. This frozen energy produces a deficiency in the flow of your life force and eventually could affect your health.

For most, the center of consciousness is located in the emotional field where the ordinary person is enslaved by thought tainted with emotions. Average humanity is submerged in the illusions of the emotional field. The emotions of anger, worry, fear, etc. create a continuous irritation of the etheric field, which affects the physical.

Emotional: relates to the element of fire and corresponds to the solar plexus chakra; externalizes as the pancreas and expresses personal power.

Mental: associated with the element of air and corresponds to the heart chakra; externalizes as the thymus gland; expresses Divine power and guides us to surrender our personal will.

Causal: relates to the element of ether and corresponds to the throat chakra; externalizes as the thyroid gland and is the field of spiritual expression.

Monadic: relates to the sixth sense and corresponds to the third oneness and integration. Externalizes as the pineal gland.

*I choose to witness my emotions and thoughts and
see when they are creating a personal story of suffering.*

Emotional Field
Keys to Happiness & Well-Being

Enlightenment

Peace

Joy

Reason

Acceptance

Willingness

Neutrality

Courage

Pride

Anger

Desire

Fear

Grief

Apathy

Guilt

Shame

*The emotional body is the field of consciousness
that contains all of your past experiences.*

When you're holding unresolved emotions from the past, your vibrations are contained in the lower frequency of the first three chakras; the root, navel and solar plexus.

Shame, guilt, apathy, anger and pride are locked into the lower chakras as emotions that haven't been healed but they have been judged and labeled.

When there is a lack of forgiveness towards others or self, then emotions stay in a frozen pattern and create toxins in your energy fields. When the heart has the capacity to do its natural work within your being such as activate the qualities of compassion, acceptance, allowing, forgiveness then the energy of the toxic emotions can be released and will move upward toward a higher consciousness of freedom and truth.

Emotions of a higher frequency such as courage, neutrality, willingness and acceptance are the beginning of emotional freedom and give rise to even greater emotions such as reason, joy, peace and enlightenment. The emotions of spiritual awakening have the quality of truth, love and beauty. They guide you to your true essence and bring true happiness.

You can observe how lower emotions affect your daily life and as they are like toxins that can be spread and shared causing much suffering in your life and others.

Remember, the downward spiral can only bring unhappiness and the upward spiral brings infinite joy and profound love.

The Temple of Your Soul - Your Akashic Light

The energy field that extends about eighteen inches beyond the mental field, in an ovoid shape that surrounds the physical field is considered the causal plane or the intuitional field. The energy of this field is radiant and full of color according to our development. It is composed of the vibrations of our soul's light and wisdom. The more evolved we become, the more luminous the colors of this energy field. This field is our sacred auric egg, or the seed body, holding the blueprint of all future incarnations.

The causal field functions as a vehicle for the true self to express the Divine law of love, wisdom and truth. The akashic records, the records of nature and stories of our soul, are held within the causal field. These stories are strung like pearls along the sacred thread, or sutratma, and bring forth the strengths and attributes the soul has acquired through all of life's experiences.

*I choose to reach for the highest frequency of the light
and to radiate this light to all beings.*

It is most urgent to use the time here on the earth plane to see that your life here is for the purpose of knowing yourself. Seek the Kingdom and you will soon realize that the Kingdom is seeking you.

The way to the Kingdom is simply living a sacred life.

This precious life teaches you the wisdom to understand the light of God which is the universal law of truth. Truth is the loving presence of God in action. The essence of this love, is the very essence of your soul. Each precious day teaches you to uncover this love - it is the art of living a sacred life.

This precious life is worthy of your time.
Allow yourself time to devote to nurturing your Divine soul.

Spirit offers these guidelines for Living a Sacred Life

- Begin each day with a prayer for all beings to live in peace.

- See that your life is for the purpose of serving God.

- Say sacred affirmations throughout your day.

- Take time each day for meditation.

- Your breath is the channel to the Divine; breathe in the Holy Spirit.

- Transcend the past through living each precious moment fully as your sacred breath.

Healing Begins with the Breath

*T*he Breath is the Light of God. When you breathe in, you receive your life force that sustains you in form. When you breathe out, you let go of energy that has been used for your body's needs and survival. Breathing takes us deeper to realize its power of sustaining not only the body, but to rejuvenate our Spirit.

To fully receive *Divine Soul Empowerment* one must learn to breathe out the energy of thought and emotions, to become an empty vessel to receive Divine Light.

Breathing out, you learn to release the psychological content of the mind; breathing in, you learn to fully embody the sacred essence of your being. You discover that through the breath of letting go, you become fully present and through the breath of receiving, you become fully embodied with your Divine energy.

The breath is the sacred pause in your life, the space between where the seed of miracles are bubbling under the surface of being. The breath allows you to fully embrace the sacred gift of life and beckons you to live your life as prayer.

The breath is the path of great mystery.

The Art of Divine Breathing

The breath is a powerful tool to realize our true nature and the Divine in all of life. The word 'pranayama' is formed from three Sanskrit roots: pra – meaning first, na – meaning energy, ayama – meaning expansion. Seeing the illusory and temporary nature of life, we can just smile and breathe out. Through the realization of our eternal being, we breathe in, affirming that awareness in all the moments of life. A slow steady breath of receiving and of letting go will guide us toward a life of peace and beauty.

Breathing in the essence of life, we learn about ourselves and listen to our body rhythm. Breathing opens our reflective consciousness and helps us to see past impressions that trap us. Exhalation can be used to let go of past psychological holding, renewing our vital force.

Improper breathing weakens the function of almost every organ in the physical body. When our breathing is shallow we become more susceptible to the full spectrum of illness – headaches, depression and constipation, emotional and mental disorders. Many researchers believe that bad breathing habits also contribute to life-threatening diseases such as cancer and heart disease. Poor breathing reduces the efficiency of the lungs, impeding oxygen flow to the cells and diminishing energy needed for normal functioning, healing and growth.

The breath is vital in supporting us in our daily challenges. Deep breathing increases our vital force; all of our senses come alive and are transformed. Our breathing gives us a spaciousness to observe where we feel heavy and where we can apply our healing light to ease unwanted burdens. Breathing takes us back to our Source and opens us up to a sense of harmony with the universal rhythm. Proper breathing clears our energy channels and opens our system to a healing light that affects all aspects of our body, mind and emotions.

The Breath and the Vital Centers

The ida, the pingala and the sushumna, the three main channels of life energy, carry the vital force to all areas of our body, mind and emotions. These channels depend on the life force breath to heal and balance the system. The ida and pingala, corresponding to the autonomic nervous system, are responsible for the maintenance of the vital essence throughout the body. The sushumna is related to the central nervous system and is the channel for the kundalini shakti. The pingala flows along the right side of the sushumna and is related to the sun. It has the yang qualities of aggression, logic, analytical thinking, outer direction, rationality, objectivity, heat, masculinity, mathematics and verbal activities. The ida flows along the left side of the sushumna and is related to the moon. It has yin qualities such as calmness, intuition, holism, inner direction, emotional subjectivity, femininity and coolness. The energy channels of the ida and pingala flow from the base chakra, weave up the spine in a snake-like manner and unite in the third eye center. The sushumna is the pathway of the breath, our Divine force that runs along the spine.

The vital centers are located along the sushumna channel and are energized by the prana they receive. Beginning in the base chakra, the breath flows upward to the solar plexus and unites with the higher prana flowing downward from the crown chakra. These two forces – the apana, meaning *"breath flowing upward"* and prana, meaning *"breath flowing downward,"* form a duality of psychic energy, creating a knot in the solar plexus chakra. This knot forms when we contract our breathing, holding on to a false identification that is rooted in suffering. Through the process of releasing our old identifications, we begin to open the sacred heart center and this knot becomes free. Breathing has a very important relationship to the opening of the heart center that serves our purpose of letting go of the past. Through our breathing we can practice this art of letting go; as we exhale we let go of the past and as we inhale we welcome the unknown mystery of life.

The Breath and Energy Field Healing

Breathing habits reflect the areas of our personal holdings and where we contract and identify with passing appearances. When we exhale we can learn to let go of all concerns and return to our natural state of contentment and stillness. When we inhale we can observe where we contract, identifying with the passing nature of life, e.g. our thoughts and emotions, and then we can return to the art of letting go through exhalation.

Within each chakra lie keys to our unfolding, and our breath carries these keys. The lower back, lower abdomen and pelvic areas carry information about our roots, our family, our origin, our survival needs and our sense of grounding. Breathing deeply into the root chakra helps to keep us feeling grounded and balanced. The navel chakra holds information about our sense of self, our relationships, physical energy and creativity. Breathing deeply, along with deep exhalations, assists our second chakra to stay balanced as well as opens us to our vital force energy. Our solar plexus chakra holds information about how we use our sense of power and helps us unite our mind with our heart.

Breathing deeply relaxes our struggle for personal power. Our throat chakra opens as we breathe in and exhale; we feel the current of energy from the lower chakras and direct this energy upward and out the crown center. When this current is flowing freely we can feel confident to speak and walk our truth. Breathing deeply and exhaling fully allows our full energy to circulate up the chakras and through the crown. Then we feel we are in a circle of vibrant light. The third eye chakra softens and opens as the pranic energy moves up and bathes the inner eye in the warm wind of our breath. The third eye chakra tells the story of who we are and where we came from to help us meet our celestial nature. Holding the stories of all our births, the crown chakra creates a crown of glory as it opens and connects with the Divine Source when we breathe deep and exhale through the crown center.

Inharmonious emotions such as anger, fear, guilt, and grief are poisons that enter our system if not released by the breath. Shallow breathing harbors these negative emotions in our energy field until there is a deep exhalation and affirmation of letting go. By observing any negative emotions or limiting thoughts that have entered our energy field, we can learn to seek the root cause and then release the disturbance through the breath.

Positive emotions and thoughts such as joy, peace, and contentment sustain our health and wellbeing. Negative emotions and thoughts create disturbances that affect our energy field, eventually leading to disease. We can learn to exhale what is no longer serving us and inhale the qualities and principles of life we need. Breathing deeply creates strength in our energy field and shields us from negative thinking. Breathing with the energy of expanding opens us to our intuitive field and allows us to meet our true nature. The art of breathing holds the key to all processes in healing the body, mind and spirit.

Conscious breathing assists us on the path of mastery, teaching us how to let go and receive our soul's wisdom. When our emotional or mental energy field is undisturbed, our breath can take us to a place of stillness, where passing thoughts and emotions are dissolved.

When undisturbed, our emotions or thoughts are like passing clouds in the sky. Breathing assists us in remaining centered and calm. Through the quiet mind we can choose peace rather than problems or conflict and release personal holdings. Our deep exhalation process provides the tools necessary to surrender the most difficult and challenging experiences.

Remaining conscious of our true nature, remembering who we are – these are essential in working with the energy fields. We then can use all of life's experience as a gift to remain in peace and harmony; our intention to live free from personal suffering.

Your Sacred Files - The Chakras

Chakra is Sanskrit for wheel of light. Each chakra is a whirling center of vital energy shaped like a cone. The chakras are found along the spinal cord or sushumna, the energetic channel that runs along the spine – from the root chakra located at the base of the spine, to the crown chakra which is at the crown of the head. The chakras energize, control and maintain proper function of our body, mind and emotions.

The chakras below the heart move in a counterclockwise manner in response to the downward pull of earth's gravity. The purpose of the lower chakras is to turn clockwise in harmony with the upper chakras. Upon awakening to our true self, the light of our consciousness pierces the center of the chakra involved and opens it to the Divine essence. Each chakra contains a lesson and has a deep and profound purpose – to assist us on our spiritual path.

These gateways to our soul are our centers of light and protection and allow accumulated energy to exist or enter the system under the direction of soul power.

Nadis are nerve-like channels that carry our spiritual and vital energies to the energy fields. Where they intersect, they form a lotus with unfolding petals – a chakra. The number of petals varies according to the number of nadis. When the chakra and the petals are facing downward, the energy is undergoing a transformative process. The transformation occurs when we learn the lessons of a particular chakra and receive the energy to proceed in the ascension process. The petals turn up as we ascend to the next level of consciousness.

When the chakras are blended and integrated they are instruments of Divine power and glory. In a state of illumination the chakras are like jewels strung along the sushumna, the life force that flows up the spine. Our chakras represent our state of consciousness and are indicators of the need to apply the healing attention of love. They are the tools for transformation, a map to our true self. We must carefully look at memories that we hold in the lower chakras.

Once we release the past, the crown chakra can take its rightful place as the master of all the others, integrating and infusing us with the Divine.

Daily Chakra Meditation & Clearing

Begin each day by scanning your energy field with you inner eye.

Take your awareness down to your **Root Chakra**
and breathe deeply saying:
"I release all fear."

"I affirm that I am in my life purpose to simply be."

Now take your awareness to the second chakra,
the **Navel Chakra**, and say:
*"I release the memory of self punishment and forgive all
experiences in my life that have contributed to a lack of self love."*

"I affirm that I love myself as a child of God."

Now bring your awareness to the **Solar Plexus Chakra** and say:
*"I release my personal power that has been used
for self-interest and self-gain."*

*"I affirm that I choose to use my power
in union with Divine will."*

Now bring your awareness to your **Heart Chakra** and say:
*"I release sorrow that has been held within my heart
so that my heart can be free to love each new moment."*

*"I affirm that this is my heart and I cherish its ability to love
more and more each day. In a higher way of service,
I choose to love myself as I love God."*

I take my attention to my **Throat Chakra** and I say:
*"I choose to forgive my expressions that are not
always in alignment with my highest truth."*

*"I affirm that I send light to my throat chakra and allow
the light to guide me to express my highest good."*

My awareness now goes to my **Third Eye Chakra** and I say:
"I choose to see that my inner eye knows the truth."

*"I affirm that I clear my vision so I may always see the truth
and always see through the eyes of God."*

I bring my attention to my **Crown Chakra** and send
light to the bridge between my Crown Chakra and
my Heaven Consciousness.

*"I affirm I am a clear channel of Divine consciousness,
ready to serve the Council of Light in the mission
of awakening and evolving love."*

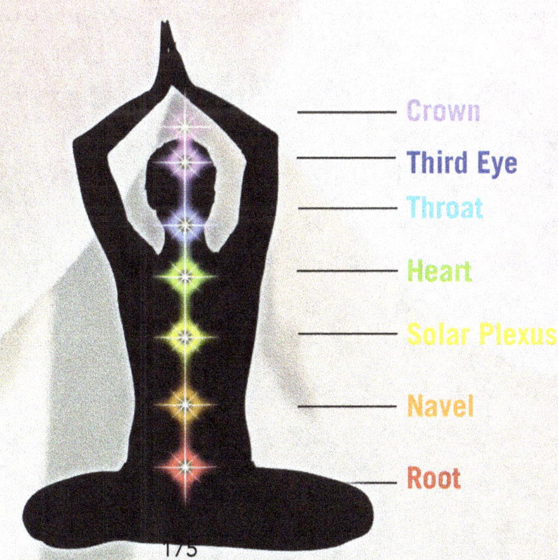

Happiness and Well-Being

Love Thyself

Sacred Inquiry is asking the questions:
Who is God? Who am I? What do I Want?

These questions lead to awakening the intelligence within, cultivating a deep and profound sense of well-being. When you listen to the observer within, you begin to know yourself as the witness. This act of listening and witnessing is the beginning of true transformation, which is the true meaning of love.

The art of happiness is to live each day as if it was the first day of the rest of your life; to begin anew and allow your spirit to live its potential without the burden of past impressions. Our true nature is revealed in happiness when we lift the veils of conditioning and reveal our inner freedom. Take a moment to visualize yourself as an empty vessel of life energy. The life energy can be understood as the wind of life blowing through you, filling you up with fresh energy, and assisting you to let go of the energy of the past. A mind that is full of ideas, perceptions and beliefs has a difficult time returning to a present state of being. However, a mind that begins the inquiry process, asking the question "Who am I," will naturally turn its attention inward to seek the answers. To inquire is to cultivate the true meaning of happiness, as the very nature of inquiry will bring a renewal of body, mind and spirit. Inquiry leads to understanding.

We can ask ourselves the fundamental questions that spark our spiritual growth. Understanding our conditioning is an important step to uncovering our natural state of happiness. Through inquiry we can see that we have been programmed through our parents' eyes to see the world in a certain way. We were told that our identification comes from our name, our status, our physical form and so on. Through our deep patterns of looking outward to define who we are, we have also become greatly affected by our outer circumstances. Seeking happiness is a natural activity of being human. The quest for finding happiness in the attainment of things, relationships, and careers is for the most part a journey shared by all of us. Through gentle observation we might come to realize that the attainment of things generally does not bring us long-lasting happiness. We may spend a great deal of our life attaining the things that we think make us happy, and then the temporary feeling of happiness wears off. We continue this search for happiness in outward things, when all along it was a search for the self. The search for our true self leads us to turn inward, contemplating the meaning of our precious life.

Our life energy is adaptable to our outer changes. It can be very joyful, mutable and free, flowing with change like a river flows through its bank. Our energy has a natural intelligence, which has a deep balancing system that works with the conditions of our life. If we know that everything is energy, we can then work with the energy of our being, learning when to practice silence, when to let go, when to fill up and when to dance with the ever-changing nature of life. Life becomes a communion bringing with it a deep sense of appreciation and gratitude, which becomes the foundation of true and long-lasting happiness. If we look at the nature of our mind we can see that a great deal of our unhappiness is caused by our thinking; by how we think about our life, our judgments and our mis-perceptions of who we are. This thinking

is the root cause of our unhappiness because of the misconceptions we have about ourselves. We measure our sense of self by the conditions of our life and our identification with our personality. As we become self-aware beings, we begin to release the patterns of misidentifica-tion and realize the true nature of our self, leading to true happiness and well-being.

As energy beings, we have the ability to perceive that we are ever evolving in love, awakening to our true essence, and aligning with the principles of God. Our inner work for true transformation of the self is to discover our life purpose and our connection with our sacred Source. This work is the foundation of our true happiness. The understanding of our true essence and our intention to evolve in love opens us to the flowering gifts of our soul such as truth, wisdom, joy, compassion, etc. Timeless happiness is realized through nourishing the true and eternal essence of self. The living qualities of God are gifts that have been given freely to us. These gifts of God bring about a positive energy flow and sustain us through life in changing experiences. The mind veiled by layers of thought, belief, and unhealed emotions resides in a state of forgetfulness. Sparks of true happiness filter through when we begin to remember our sacred Source.

What Defines True Happiness?

We know we are happy when we have achieved a sense of peace, and when we are not so prone to reaction, frustration, and irritability. We seem to have gone through a genuine transformation where we no longer put all our value in the temporary conditions of our life. We have turned our attention inward and we nourish our sacred being with the seeds of true happiness. This transformation is real love that we cultivate by disengaging from all the energies that do not contribute to our well-being. We simply decide to stop contributing to our own suffering and the suffering of others. Time becomes a precious commodity when we understand deeply that this life is very short and we dedicate our moments to be free from self-inflicted suffering. Understanding the nature of the mind can guide us to the art of true happiness. We can see how our mind swings in the polarities between pain and pleasure, gain and loss. We begin the path to our true awakening by realizing that happiness is not in what we gain, but in the peace and observation of the eternal nature of life. This realization is discovered by quieting our minds and discovering the world of our inner being that is filled with joy, light and wisdom.

Create an intention for Well-Being

Living an intentional life is walking the path of mindfulness and becoming the self-aware being we are in truth. It is making a choice to no longer live in the lower frequencies of gain and loss, pleasure and pain, in the identification of the self-centered "I" thought. It is living an intention to be of service and that, in truth, happiness is each human's birthright. The intention or direction for your life has a deep connection with your understanding of love – love that is beyond self-gratification and is founded in the desire to serve, which is cultivated by compassion. Love is nourished by looking to something higher for guidance, which can be discovered through meditation and practicing inquiry. This inner practice leads to the awakening of the true self within, which is revealed as a multifaceted diamond of great brilliance. You are simply an energy being and your inner work is to allow for expansion and to open to your highest potential.

Happiness is the true nature of your soul, the childlike innocence of your being. When there is unhappiness, it is because of forgetting who you are and believing in the temporary conditions of your life experience. The circumstances of your life change and will continue to change throughout. But what is it that remains free, witnessing your life?

Do you have compassion for this suffering world?
Do you have compassion for your own suffering?

When compassion is developed then there is a deeper chance to serve. In this chance, one looks at the possibilities of living without harm to oneself and others. These are the stepping stones to true happiness. This path of soul development leads to the understanding and wisdom that our life is not here just for our self-gain, but it is truly to help others on the path and to remember God.

Steps to Happiness and Well-Being

1. **Practice letting go.** Allow yourself to let go of accumulated thoughts, beliefs, and emotions.

2. **Create a spiritual practice**, one that cultivates compassion, forgiveness, acceptance, and service.

3. **Understand the true Source of happiness.** Know that true happiness comes from love, which transforms the Source of unhappiness.

4. **Release resistance.** Let go of what holds you back from being in the now.

5. **Discover the observer.** Watch the patterns of your thoughts, judgments and reactions. Observe how this affects your happiness.

6. **Remember your true self.** When there is unhappiness there is often a sense of forgetting. Simply turn the attention inward and through contemplation, joy returns.

7. **Practice "Yes" breathing.** Breathe and relax into the contracted thoughts and emotions while setting clear intentions for well-being.

8. **Discover sacred alignment.** A process in which your higher self observes the energetic patterns that are not bringing you joy and well-being. Releasing them infuses your being with the qualities of spirit; Divine love, joy, compassion and truth.

9. **Your natural state is of well-being.** The only hindrance to your natural state of well-being comes from accumulated thoughts and emotions that are based on misidentification and conditioning.

10. **Loving yourself.** Through remembering your Source, you will naturally and intelligently begin to realize who you are and that loving yourself also loves your sacred Source of God.

11. **Resonating with joy.** The mind, when full of thoughts and emotions without intention to evolve in love, is a mind that has a hard time allowing joy. When the mind is silent, full of innocence and childlike wonder, joy becomes a natural part of daily life.

12. **Creative life flow.** The creative impulses of your life are the sparks that keep you alive and your energy flowing. Welcome them. Creating with Source can be as simple as writing in a journal, painting, walking, dancing or anything that brings you joyful anticipation.

13. **Emotional well-being.** Feeling emotionally well is to pay attention to your frequency. When your emotions drop down you will feel it in your body. You can learn to raise your frequency through affirming gratitude, joy, appreciation and unconditional love for all your life's experience.

14. **Acceptance and understanding.** When you understand, you can also let go of your need to be right, and you can allow life to be what it is. Staying present in this welcoming space and allowing for acceptance is the key to happiness, which is what leads to peace.

15. **Realize you are lovable and you are simply a child of God.** Because you have lived in a state of separation, you hold deep feelings of abandonment, shame and guilt. You fear that you are not enough and often seek to become something more. This is rooted once again in the mistaken identification that you are your body, mind, emotions, and all the conditions of your life.

16. **Reconnect and realign with what is real, the Source of true happiness.** Just opening to the possibility of a Divine Source is a first step in reconnection. The energy of your sacred life will sigh in relief as you open to its magnificence. You will immediately feel a change and an increase in frequency. Your thoughts and emotions will align with the principles of the Divine and you will naturally experience your life gifts of joy, happiness, peace, compassion, wisdom and unconditional love.

17. **Taking responsibility for your sacred journey.** At some point, you will decide to let go of blame and shame in your relationships. You will no longer hold others responsible for your experience. This is a profound step to personal empowerment and the art of true happiness.

The Sacred Yes!

Energy is dynamically expansive, flowing and moving with positive intention. The Sacred **Yes** is when you live without resistance, which is truly living in peace, and acceptance of what is. The Sacred **Yes** is a force that guides you to your potential. It is a way of being that allows you to be free to say **Yes** to what life is asking of you: to be of service to life.

Through practicing **Yes** you will find that life becomes a reflection of that and your deepest heart's wishes begin to come true. When there are negative thoughts and emotions, take a moment to scan your energy body. Notice where there is contraction, control, fear and other dissonant feelings. As soon as you allow the contracted emotions or thoughts to flow freely, you move back into the feeling of **Yes**; a positive energy flow of intention.

Section V

Divine Soul Meditations

*This section offers you 3 powerful guided meditations
for you to use as needed to nurture your Divine soul.*

Invoking the Light

Receive the Gifts of the Divine

A Journey of Ascension to Your Higher Self

Invoking the Light

Breathe deeply each morning and each evening
so you may call in the Divine guidance for your life.

Take a moment and offer your heart to the Beloved.

Offer all your thoughts and emotions to the altar of the Divine.

Ask that your personal story be aligned with the greatest story
of your soul. Know you have the goodness of all of God's creation
available to you.

You simply must release any doubts or feelings of
unworthiness, as you are a child of God.

Meditate daily within your inner temple and you will
manifest your life's dreams.

Spend moments of your day to unite with the Divine.
Your life is a miracle of unfolding love.

Receive the Gifts of the Divine

Life is a movement of giving energy to the temporary nature of change. Time goes by and we forget to breathe in the miracle of life.

Breathing in, allow your crown chakra to open to receive the Holy vibration of your Source.

Breathing out, release the effort of personal striving.

Just for a moment rest in silence and receive the unmanifested gift of presence.

Know that you have within your inner treasure box all the gifts of the Divine that will bring you ever-lasting happiness and peace.

A Journey of Ascension
to Your Higher Self

*M*editate on your ascension each day. See a white light traveling through your spine, releasing all the built up debris from accumulated thought and emotion.

This white light is your Divine power tool to clear your karma and free your life force so it can unify with your Source. The spine is your tube of light that must be clear so energy can flow freely.

Scan your energy daily so you can learn to sense when your tube
of light is heavy with the lower frequency of the world's vibration.

Reach for the stars with your hands and then release your hands back to earth.

Open your arms to the Divine, then bring your arms to your
heart with deep gratitude.

Visualize white light flowing down the front of your energy field
and coming up the back of your body in a circle of Divine protection.

This is your breath of restoration, your true nature will shine in its luminous light.

Afterword

Desiderata

GO PLACIDLY amid the noise and the haste, and remember
what peace there may be in silence.

As far as possible, without surrender, be on good terms with all persons.

Speak your truth quietly and clearly; and listen to others,
even to the dull and the ignorant; they too have their story.

Avoid loud and aggressive persons; they are vexatious to the spirit.
If you compare yourself with others, you may become vain or bitter,
for always there will be greater and lesser persons than yourself.

Enjoy your achievements as well as your plans.
Keep interested in your own career, however humble;
it is a real possession in the changing fortunes of time.

Exercise caution in your business affairs, for the world is full of trickery.
But, let this not blind you to what virtue there is; many persons strive for
high ideals, and everywhere life is full of heroism.

Be yourself. Especially do not feign affection.
Neither be cynical about love; for in the face of all aridity
and disenchantment, it is as perennial as the grass.

Take kindly the counsel of the years,
gracefully surrendering the things of youth.

Nurture strength of spirit to shield you in sudden misfortune.
But, do not distress yourself with dark imaginings.
Many fears are born of fatigue and loneliness.

Beyond a wholesome discipline, be gentle with yourself.
You are a child of the universe no less than the trees and the stars;
you have a right to be here.

And whether or not it is clear to you, no doubt the universe is
unfolding as it should. Therefore, be at peace with God, whatever you conceive
Him to be. And whatever your labors and aspirations, in the noisy confusion of
life, keep peace in your soul. With all its sham, drudgery and broken dreams,
it is still a beautiful world. Be cheerful. Strive to be happy.

The Divine Team

Jaya Sarada

Jaya is the author of many transformational books; she brings to her work a lifetime of devotion and service. In her ever-evolving work, she offers profound Divine transmissions, inspired guidance, and light of being leading you to your Source of true Divine Empowerment.

Jaya Sarada has devoted her life to self inquiry, witnessing and healing the cause of suffering in her own life and all those who request her help. She has studied the anatomy of the soul and understands all is energy. In her work she offers deep healing for your soul and a sacred time that invites a communion with your Divine Source. Through healing touch, affirmations, sound and invocation to the light she becomes a channel for the Divine. These profound and life changing sessions assist you to let go of the past and experience a soul renewal, uncovering the radiant light of your being. It is through Holy Grace, deep surrender and entering the sanctuary of your silent being, you meet that which has always been present, the witness, the beautiful, loving soul that you are. In this meeting there is profound joy.

Jaya has been channeling the "Council of Light" for over 10 years and offers their beautiful messages in her books; *Trust in Yourself, Living Meditations, The Sacred Path of Love, The Sacred Path of Peace* and her most recent book *Divine Soul Empowerment.* Jaya is available for private sessions, telephone readings, personal retreats and classes.

For more information see jayasarada.com.

Arielle Beauduy
Co-Creator, Project Manager & Editor

I am a digital marketing consultant who focuses on working with companies that have a unique vision and a sincere desire to share their valuable gifts with the world. I am also Jaya's daughter and have been blessed to be immersed in global spiritual teachings since I was very young. I have worked with Jaya on many of her transformational books. I believe when we all support and share our gifts we create nurturing communities, we fuel inspiration, and we help bring a greater awareness to the world.

Patricia Frances
Spiritual Guide, Teacher & Editor

I am a Buddhist who seemed fated to meet an extraordinary, learned lama who'd escaped from Tibet, traversed over the Himalayas and just happened to be passing through my home town on Orcas Island. A meeting was arranged, and I was able to take my Buddhist and Bodhisattva vows during which time Rinpoche cleared my mind and brought home the truths about the essential nature of reality. Any seeking came to a stunning conclusion. I find this to be the possibility of *Divine Soul Empowerment*. It is filled with wisdom of the ages and all one need do is to breathe deeply into some quiet time and simply take in each beautiful page and see if your mind, body, heart and soul begin to re-awaken to original pure consciousness. The lessons that were transmitted through Jaya combined with the spectacular graphics are profoundly moving. Let us move in the world with a fierce faith in our innate goodness and a recognition of the Divine in each other.

The Divine Team

Dianne Leonetti-Rux

Creative Director - Graphic Designer
dzinergraphics.com - diannedziner@gmail.com

I have been instrumental in the development and creation of the Divine Light Books, and the books written by Jaya Sarada. Entrenched in the world of design, I've worked with clients from around the world, but for the past 10 years, my main focus has been my devotion to Jaya and the wonderful works Jaya has brought to the world.

As an award winning graphic designer, and skilled in marketing, advertising and book publishing, I am proud to bring my talents to Divine Light Publishing. I am extremely grateful that I am able to assist in sharing this valuable and inspiring work with all enlightened souls.

I have owned and launched a number of magazines; *Las Vegas Image Magazine, Creative Independent Artists (CIA Magazine), V.I.P. Magazine, "I" Magazine*, as well as many other best-selling books nationwide. But, Jaya's work has been a mainstay in my life for the past 10 years and working with her has been a joy and an inspiration.

Shannon Pocan

Editor, Assistant Manager

I am an intuitive oracle, tarot, and aura reader, empath, graphic designer, amateur astrologer, lover, and all around co-creator with this beautiful Universe.

Through sharing our stories, we start to see the intersections where we all meet. Through love and compassion, we start to see the fullness inside of us. Through passion and service, we start to become authentically ourselves. As we remove ourselves from duality we start to see how connected we all are to each other and to Source.

My mission in this life is to help people see their own inner light and love; to discover the beautiful Source energy that exists beyond our physical reality that is inside of us always. We have each been given such a beautiful opportunity to experience life and to experience God. My wish for you is to know that you are, and always have been, worthy of being your most authentic self.

This being human is a guest house.
Every morning a new arrival.
A joy, a depression, a meanness,
some momentary awareness comes
as an unexpected visitor.

Welcome and entertain them all!
Even if they're a crowd of sorrows,
who violently sweep your house
empty of its furniture,
still, treat each guest honorably.

He may be clearing you out
for some new delight.

The dark thought, the shame, the malice,
meet them at the door laughing,
and invite them in.

Be grateful for whoever comes,
because each has been sent
as a guide from beyond.

Rumi

Divine Soul Empowerment
Living in the Light

Divine Soul Empowerment - Living in the Light is the work of Jaya Sarada and Arielle Beauduy. We offer workshops, retreats, guided meditations and *Soul Empowerment Sessions*. These guided experiences are enlivened with meditations, sacred inquiry, journaling, movement, sound healing and sacred chanting.

Our *Divine Oracle,* is a deck of 44 inspired cards that include 11 Divine Gifts with 33 Sacred Messages to be used daily as a guide for your awakening and well being. The book, journal and oracle serve as a means for your path of transcendence, healing and awakening.

The *Divine Soul Empowerment Journal and Book-Living in the Light* will take you on a journey of self discovery, prompting you to awaken your soul's truth and to nurture the light of your being. It is through quiet contemplation that we uncover who we really are, and are rejuvenated with the grace of life. Within this inspired book and journal, you will find questions that will lead you to contemplate the purpose of your life. You will be guided to write down your soul's truth, spending quiet moments to let go of what is no longer serving you. The *Divine Soul Empowerment Book and Journal* are filled with inspirational quotes from spiritual teachers throughout the world.

For more information or to contact us:
DivineSoulEmpowerment.com
email: events@divinesoulempowerment.com
1.855.505.3935

* 9 7 8 1 8 9 3 0 3 7 5 9 5 *